PIANO | VOC...

Boublil and Schönberg's Legendary Musical

Les Misérables

Book, Music and Lyrics by Alain Boublil and Claude-Michel Schönberg
English Lyrics by Herbert Kretzmer

Dramatic Performance rights controlled and licensed by
Cameron Mackintosh (Overseas) Ltd.
One Bedford Square, London WC1B 3RA England
Tel (20) 7637 8866 Fax (20) 7436 2683

Stock and Amateur Performance Rights are licensed by
Musical Theater International, Inc.
545 Eighth Avenue, New York, New York 10018
Tel (212) 868-6668 Fax (212) 643-8465

Non-Dramatic and Concert Performance Rights are controlled by
Alain Boublil Music Ltd. and licensed by the American Society of
Composers, Authors and Publishers (ASCAP), One Lincoln Plaza,
New York, New York 10023
Tel (212) 595-3050 Fax (212) 787-1381

ISBN 0-634-08742-8

ALAIN BOUBLIL MUSIC LTD.

c/o Joel Faden and Company Inc., 1775 Broadway, New York, NY 10019

7777 W. BLUEMOUND RD. P.O. BOX 13819 MILWAUKEE, WI 53213

Visit Hal Leonard Online at
www.halleonard.com

CONTENTS

BRING HIM HOME

Music by CLAUDE-MICHEL SCHÖNBERG
Lyrics by ALAIN BOUBLIL and HERBERT KRETZMER

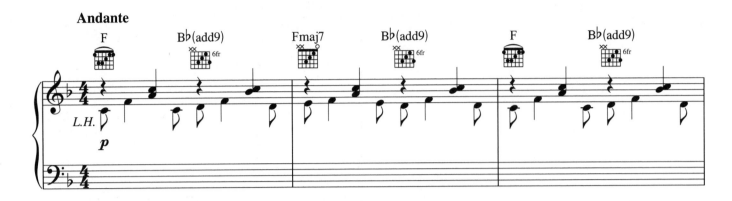

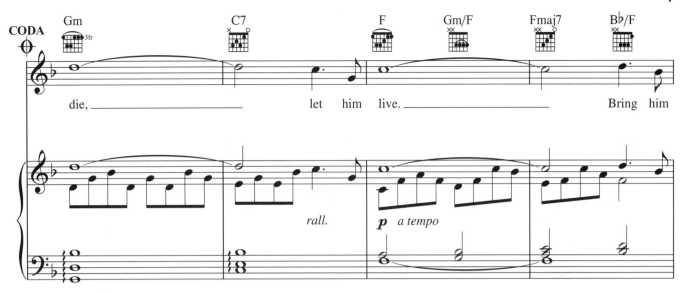

CODA

die, _____ let him live. _____ Bring him

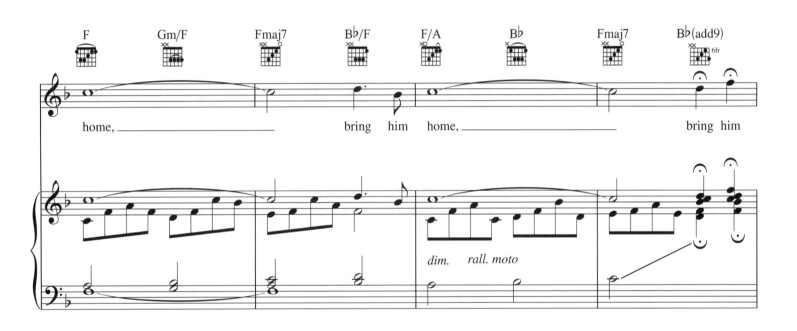

home, _____ bring him home, _____ bring him

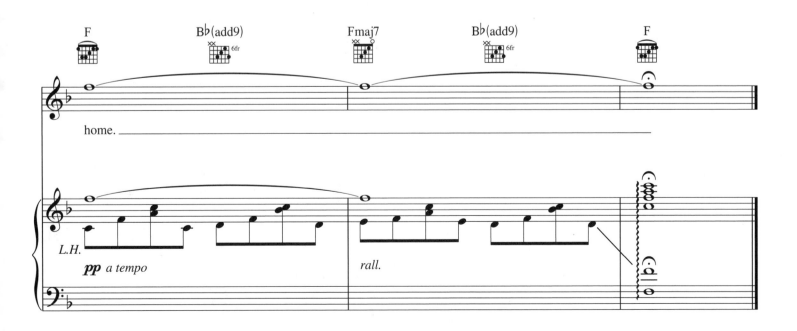

home. _____

CASTLE ON A CLOUD

Music by CLAUDE-MICHEL SCHÖNBERG
Lyrics by ALAIN BOUBLIL, JEAN MARC NATEL
and HERBERT KRETZMER

COSETTE:

There is a cas - tle on a cloud.
There is a room that's full of toys.

I like to go there in my sleep.
There are a hun - dred boys and girls.

DO YOU HEAR THE PEOPLE SING?

Music by CLAUDE-MICHEL SCHÖNBERG
Lyrics by ALAIN BOUBLIL, JEAN MARC NATEL
and HERBERT KRETZMER

DRINK WITH ME
(To Days Gone By)

Music by CLAUDE-MICHEL SCHÖNBERG
Lyrics by HERBERT KRETZMER and ALAIN BOUBLIL

FEUILLY:

Drink with me to days gone by.
me to days gone by.
me to days gone by,

Sing with me the songs we knew.
Can it be you fear to die?
To the life that used to be.

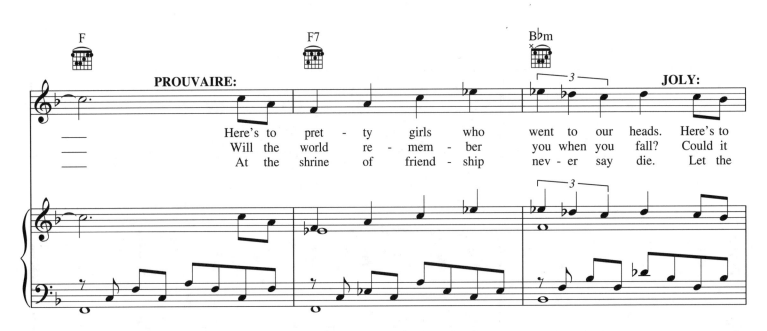

PROUVAIRE:

Here's to pretty girls who went to our heads. Here's to
Will the world remember you when you fall? Could it
At the shrine of friendship never say die. Let the

JOLY:

EMPTY CHAIRS AT EMPTY TABLES

Music by CLAUDE-MICHEL SCHÖNBERG
Lyrics by ALAIN BOUBLIL and HERBERT KRETZMER

Moderato

MARIUS:

There's a grief that can't be

spo - ken. _____ There's a pain goes on and on. _____

Emp - ty chairs at emp - ty ta - bles, now my friends are dead and

ON MY OWN

Music by CLAUDE-MICHEL SCHÖNBERG
Lyrics by ALAIN BOUBLIL, JOHN CAIRD,
TREVOR NUNN, JEAN-MARC NATEL
and HERBERT KRETZMER

I DREAMED A DREAM

Music by CLAUDE-MICHEL SCHÖNBERG
Lyrics by ALAIN BOUBLIL,
JEAN-MARC NATEL and HERBERT KRETZMER

A LITTLE FALL OF RAIN

Music by CLAUDE-MICHEL SCHÖNBERG
Lyrics by ALAIN BOUBLIL,
JEAN-MARC NATEL and HERBERT KRETZMER

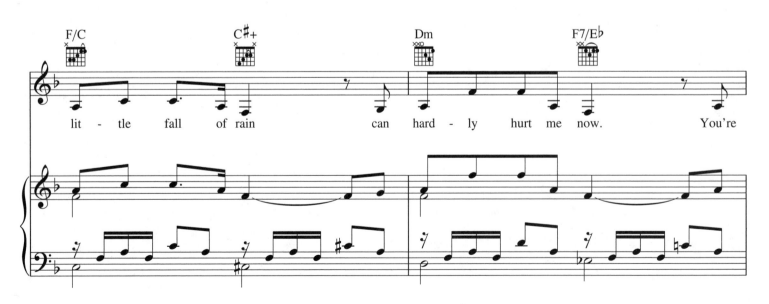

EPONINE:
Don't you fret, M'sieur Marius, I don't feel any pain. A little fall of rain can hardly hurt me now. You're

THE ULTIMATE SONGBOOKS

PIANO PLAY-ALONG

These great songbook/CD packs come with our standard arrangements for piano and voice with guitar chord frames plus a CD. The CD includes a full performance of each song, as well as a second track without the piano part so you can play "lead" with the band!

Vol. 1 Movie Music
Come What May • Forrest Gump – Main Title (Feather Theme) • My Heart Will Go On (Love Theme from *Titanic*) • The Rainbow Connection • Tears in Heaven • A Time for Us • Up Where We Belong • Where Do I Begin (Love Theme).
00311072 P/V/G......................$12.95

Vol. 2 Jazz Ballads
Autumn in New York • Do You Know What It Means to Miss New Orleans • Georgia on My Mind • In a Sentimental Mood • More Than You Know • The Nearness of You • The Very Thought of You • When Sunny Gets Blue.
00311073 P/V/G......................$12.95

Vol. 3 Timeless Pop
Ebony and Ivory • Every Breath You Take • From a Distance • I Write the Songs • In My Room • Let It Be • Oh, Pretty Woman • We've Only Just Begun.
00311074 P/V/G......................$12.95

Vol. 4 Broadway Classics
Ain't Misbehavin' • Cabaret • If I Were a Bell • Memory • Oklahoma • Some Enchanted Evening • The Sound of Music • You'll Never Walk Alone.
00311075 P/V/G......................$12.95

Vol. 5 Disney
Beauty and the Beast • Can You Feel the Love Tonight • Colors of the Wind • Go the Distance • Look Through My Eyes • A Whole New World • You'll Be in My Heart • You've Got a Friend in Me.
00311076 P/V/G......................$12.95

Vol. 6 Country Standards
Blue Eyes Crying in the Rain • Crazy • King of the Road • Oh, Lonesome Me • Ring of Fire • Tennessee Waltz • You Are My Sunshine • Your Cheatin' Heart.
00311077 P/V/G......................$12.95

Vol. 7 Love Songs
Can't Help Falling in Love • (They Long to Be) Close to You • Here, There and Everywhere • How Deep Is Your Love • I Honestly Love You • Maybe I'm Amazed • Wonderful Tonight • You Are So Beautiful.
00311078 P/V/G......................$12.95

Vol. 8 Classical Themes
Can Can • Habanera • Humoresque • In the Hall of the Mountain King • Minuet in G Major • Piano Concerto No. 21 in C Major, 2nd Movement Excerpt • Prelude in E Minor, Op. 28, No. 4 • Symphony No. 5 in C Minor, 1st Movement Excerpt.
00311079 Piano Solo..............$12.95

Vol. 9 Children's Songs
Do-Re-Mi • It's a Small World • Linus and Lucy • Sesame Street Theme • Sing • Winnie the Pooh • Won't You Be My Neighbor? • Yellow Submarine.
0311080 P/V/G........................$12.95

Vol. 10 Wedding Classics
Air on the G String • Ave Maria • Bridal Chorus • Canon in D • Jesu, Joy of Man's Desiring • Ode to Joy • Trumpet Voluntary • Wedding March.
00311081 Piano Solo...............$12.95

Vol. 11 Wedding Favorites
All I Ask of You • Don't Know Much • Endless Love • Grow Old with Me • In My Life • Longer • Wedding Processional • You and I.
00311097 P/V/G........................$12.95

Vol. 12 Christmas Favorites
Blue Christmas • The Christmas Song • Do You Hear What I Hear • Here Comes Santa Claus • I Saw Mommy Kissing Santa Claus • Let It Snow! Let It Snow! Let It Snow! • Merry Christmas, Darling • Silver Bells.
00311137 P/V/G........................$12.95

Vol. 13 Yuletide Favorites
Angels We Have Heard on High • Away in a Manger • Deck the Hall • The First Noel • Go, Tell It on the Mountain • Jingle Bells • Joy to the World • O Little Town of Bethlehem.
00311138 P/V/G......................$12.95

Vol. 14 Pop Ballads
Have I Told You Lately • I'll Be There for You • It's All Coming Back to Me Now • Looks Like We Made It • Rainy Days and Monday • Say You, Say Me • She's Got a Way • Your Song.
00311145 P/V/G......................$12.95

Vol. 15 Favorite Standards
Call Me • The Girl from Ipanema • Moon River • My Way • Satin Doll • Smoke Gets in Your Eyes • Strangers in the Night • The Way You Look Tonight.
00311146 P/V/G......................$12.95

Vol. 16 TV Classics
The Brady Bunch • Green Acres Theme • Happy Days • Johnny's Theme • Love Boat Theme • Mister Ed • The Munsters Theme • Where Everybody Knows Your Name.
00311147 P/V/G......................$12.95

Vol. 17 Movie Favorites
Back to the Future • Theme from E.T. • Footloose • For All We Know • Somewhere in Time • Somewhere Out There • Theme from *Terms of Endearment* • You Light Up My Life.
00311148 P/V/G......................$12.95

Vol. 18 Jazz Standards
All the Things You Are • Bluesette • Easy Living • I'll Remember April • Isn't It Romantic? • Stella by Starlight • Tangerine • Yesterdays.
00311149 P/V/G......................$12.95

Vol. 19 Contemporary Hits
Beautiful • Calling All Angels • Don't Know Why • If I Ain't Got You • 100 Years • This Love • A Thousand Miles • You Raise Me Up.
00311162 P/V/G......................$12.95

Vol. 20 R&B Ballads
After the Love Has Gone • All in Love Is Fair • Hello • I'll Be There • Let's Stay Together • Midnight Train to Georgia • Tell It like It Is • Three Times a Lady.
00311163 P/V/G......................$12.95

Vol. 21 Big Bands
All or Nothing at All • Apple Honey • April in Paris • Cherokee • In the Mood • Opus One • Stardust • Stompin' at the Savoy.
00311164 P/V/G......................$12.95

Vol. 22 Rock Classics
Against All Odds • Bennie and the Jets • Come Sail Away • Do It Again • Free Bird • Jump • Wanted Dead or Alive • We Are the Champions.
00311165 P/V/G......................$12.95

Vol. 23 Worship Classics
Awesome God • How Majestic Is Your Name • Lord, Be Glorified • Lord, I Lift Your Name on High • Praise the Name of Jesus • Shine, Jesus, Shine • Step by Step • There Is a Redeemer.
00311166 P/V/G......................$12.95

Vol. 24 Les Misérables
Bring Him Home • Castle on a Cloud • Do You Hear the People Sing? • Drink with Me • Empty Chairs at Empty Tables • I Dreamed a Dream • A Little Fall of Rain • On My Own.
00311169 P/V/G......................$12.95

Vol. 25 The Sound of Music
Climb Ev'ry Mountain • Do-Re-Mi • Edelweiss • Maria • My Favorite Things • Sixteen Going on Seventeen • Something Good • The Sound of Music.
00311175 P/V/G......................$12.95

Vol. 26 Andrew Lloyd Webber Favorites
All I Ask of You • Amigos Para Siempre • As If We Never Said Goodbye • Everything's Alright • Memory • No Matter What • Tell Me on a Sunday • You Must Love Me.
00311178 P/V/G......................$12.95

Vol. 27 Andrew Lloyd Webber Greats
Any Dream Will Do • Don't Cry for Me Argentina • I Don't Know How to Love Him • The Music of the Night • The Phantom of the Opera • Unexpected Song • Whistle Down the Wind • With One Look.
00311179 P/V/G......................$12.95

Vol. 29 The Beach Boys
Barbara Ann • Be True to Your School • California Girls • Fun, Fun, Fun • Help Me Rhonda • I Get Around • Little Deuce Coupe • Wouldn't It Be Nice.
00311181 P/V/G......................$12.95

Vol. 30 Elton John
Candle in the Wind • Crocodile Rock • Daniel • Goodbye Yellow Brick Road • I Guess That's Why They Call It the Blues • Levon • Sorry Seems to Be the Hardest Word • Your Song.
00311182 P/V/G......................$12.95

Vol. 35 Elvis Presley Hits
Blue Suede Shoes • Can't Help Falling in Love • Don't Be Cruel (To a Heart That's True) • Heartbreak Hotel • I Want You, I Need You, I Love You • It's Now or Never • Love Me • (Let Me Be Your) Teddy Bear.
00311230 P/V/G......................$12.95

Vol. 36 Elvis Presley Greats
All Shook Up • Don't • Jailhouse Rock • Love Me Tender • Loving You • Return to Sender • Too Much • Wooden Heart .
00311231 P/V/G......................$12.95

Disney characters and artwork
© Disney Enterprises, Inc.

FOR MORE INFORMATION, SEE YOUR LOCAL MUSIC DEALER, OR WRITE TO:

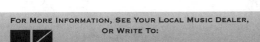

7777 W. BLUEMOUND RD. P.O. BOX 13819 MILWAUKEE, WI 53213

Visit Hal Leonard Online at **www.halleonard.com**

Prices, contents and availability subject to change without notice.

0605